Three Men Filled with the Spirit

The gift of Tongues: must it divide us?

MICHAEL C. GRIFFITHS

General Director of the
Overseas Missionary Fellowship

OMF BOOKS ◇ LONDON

© OVERSEAS MISSIONARY FELLOWSHIP

First published	..	.. *November 1969*
Reprinted ..	..	.. *March 1970*
Reprinted ..	..	.. *September 1970*
Reprinted ..	..	.. *July 1971*
Reprinted ..	..	.. *November 1972*
Reprinted ..	..	.. *1974*
Reprinted ..	..	.. *February 1975*

Biblical quotations are from the Revised Standard Version
unless otherwise stated. Copyright 1946 by the Division of
Christian Education of the National Council of Churches of
Christ in the USA.

ISBN 85363 073 9

Made in Great Britain
Published by Overseas Missionary Fellowship
Newington Green, London, N 16 9QD
and printed offset by the Camelot Press Ltd.,
Southampton

PREFACE TO THE FIFTH PRINTING

A preface seems necessary to contradict the circulation of false rumours to the effect that I have 'changed my mind' (and the same thing has been falsely asserted of others). I do not have the impression that the danger of over-emphasis has passed. There are fair-minded, moderate people on both sides, but there are extreme people on both sides as well. If any change in my thinking on this subject has taken place since this book was first written, it is one of deepening regret that unbalanced, extreme teaching has not yet been banished from our midst.

I have no difficulty with a truly Biblical charismatic emphasis, that seeks to recover spiritual gifts for a much-needed deepening of worship and development of a genuine congregational life. The letters addressed to the Corinthian congregation manifestly do not intend to assert that every single member should seek for the gift of tongues, which could encourage mere self-congratulation, but rather that all should seek earnestly the best gifts for congregational edification: not that I should have a gift, but that *we* should, i.e. that some one or more individuals might possess that gift for the mutual benefit of the whole body. The problem arises only because we read the Epistle as though it were addressed to an individual, instead of to a congregation. There is no difficulty then about some in the congregation having the gift of tongues, provided it is exercised within the limits which Scripture lays down. The difficulty arises when it is asserted that all may, or should, or that it is desirable that all should, speak in tongues.

My problem then is with those hyper-charismatics who, albeit inadvertently, are teaching a mandatory second experience for every believer, sometimes referred to as 'the baptism in the Spirit', generally marked by the outward and visible sign of being able to speak in tongues. Whatever is said to the contrary, the inevitable result is to divide Christians into two classes: those with, and those without that experience. The danger is, albeit unintentionally, to develop a neo-Gnostic in-group. Colossians was written to insist that 'Christ among you' is the secret, because all the riches and fulness are in Christ alone, and He indwells the whole congregation, and not just a specially initiated segment of it. Full salvation to the hyper-charismatics becomes Christ plus the Second experience, and Galatians was written to show that Christ plus anything, makes that 'anything' the decisive and essential ingredient.

Paul's aim in the Corinthian letters was manifestly to place controls upon the *public* use of the gift of tongues, yet verses are taken from this context as though Paul was intending to teach a *private* use of tongues. We do not seem to have an explicit account of anyone in the New Testament speaking in tongues privately: at best it is a possible *deduction* from Paul's statements that he spoke in tongues (languages?) more than all, but preferred five words that are understandable to ten thousand words in a tongue (foreign language?). There are many doctrines, which when once assumed can be defended as consonant with Scripture which would never have been arrived at starting with Scripture alone.

Many of us have waited to see evidence of the fruits of this emphasis—and in some cases have rejoiced to see effective evangelism, fruitful ministry and radiant changed lives, coupled with a quiet, unpublicized experience and undogmatic conviction. But we have also been disturbed by devious and divisive hyper-charismatic teaching, so that whole conferences, societies and publishing ventures have been formed to propagate the over-emphasis. May I repeat then, speaking as an individual, that the chief change in my thinking is deepening regret that unbalanced and extreme teaching has not yet been corrected and banished from our midst.

London   M. C. GRIFFITHS
November 1972

INTRODUCTION

This book is the substance of three papers given to a group of missionaries in November 1968 and published at their request. In preparing them it was my prayer that the studies would make some contribution towards greater mutual toleration between those of opposing views, and that Christians who have been disunited on the matter of 'speaking in tongues' might come to one mind and one heart.

In presenting this material in book form now, my aims are fivefold:

(i) Christians are urged to strive 'to maintain the unity of the Spirit in the bond of peace' (Eph. 4:3). I assume this to mean that we should take active steps to avoid division and faction between Christians. We are not only to refrain from being divisive; nor are we to be merely passive; but we are to take active steps to keep Christians in 'the unity of the Spirit'. The way in which people on both sides of the controversy have spoken of 'the gift of tongues' has tended to be divisive, and this cannot be right.

(ii) My aim is *not* to demonstrate that a particular view either for or against 'speaking in tongues' is the *only* legitimate Scriptural position. It is, however, to show that there is strong Biblical support for what one may call, for want of a better word, 'the traditional evangelical view'; also that there are other Scriptures, the interpretation of which, while not conclusive, *may* be consonant with that spectrum of theology known as 'Neo-Pentecostalism'. My purpose is *not* to exclude either position, but to show that, because both interpretations are Scripturally arguable, those who espouse either view should not espouse them in such a way as to break the unity of the Spirit. Moreover, no one should denigrate those who hold an opposing view as either mistaken Christians chasing a spiritual will-o'-the-wisp on the one hand, or as inferior Christians missing an essential experience on the other. It is not my intention to question the reality of anyone's experience, but only to question the interpretation which some have sought to place upon their experience.

(iii) In order to avoid an arid controversial approach, I have tried to present the material not only in a theological, but also in a devotional manner. We ought never merely to argue about what Scripture says, but ought also to rejoice in and benefit from what it tells us about the Lord Himself and all that He gives. This book then takes the form of studies of three men filled with the Spirit: Peter, Paul and Stephen, all of them men whose example we would wish to follow.

(iv) Every one of us, irrespective of our position on 'tongues', wants to enjoy all the blessings that are ours in Christ Jesus, and that are set before us in prospect in the Bible. Every one of us longs that Paul's prayer in Ephesians 3 should be fulfilled in our experience. Whatever our view about 'the baptism of the Spirit' or 'speaking in tongues', every one of us longs that we may be 'strengthened with might through His Spirit in the inner man' (3:16). Every one of us, hollow men and women that we are, longs to 'be filled with all the fullness of God' (3:19). If the New Testament says this is possible, this is what we all want.

There are extremes which we wish to avoid, like the Scylla and Charybdis between which Ulysses had to sail. On the one hand, there is the danger of so magnifying doctrine about the Holy Spirit that we go beyond the Scriptures; that we talk more about the Spirit than about Christ Himself; that we run to the excessive subjectivism of the Quakers, who make experience the supreme authority; or that we make exaggerated claims (subsequently to be discredited) like the Irvingites. It is dangerously possible to add to the Bible interpretations, fancies and elaborations of our own. It is possible to find some justification from Scripture for what we have come to believe *from experience*, but we should not necessarily have arrived at our conclusions if we had begun with the Bible teaching itself.

At the other extremity some Christians are so fearful of what they regard as 'extreme' that they denigrate the New Testament doctrine and are in danger of overlooking or ignoring certain passages of Scripture. They omit to give full weight to what the New Testament has to say about the gifts of the Spirit and speaking in tongues; they may even become suspicious when the Holy Spirit is mentioned lest the mention implies a view with which they disagree. Without the Holy Spirit there is no Christianity. It is the Holy Spirit who helps us to understand the Bible, to preach the Gospel, to pray to God. It is the Holy Spirit who changes us from one degree of glory to another into the likeness of Christ (2 Cor. 3:18). Those whom the Spirit calls He also justifies, and them He also glorifies (Rom. 8:30). 'The God who has begun a good work in us will complete it in the day of Jesus Christ without a doubt I am certain' (runs a free translation of the Japanese version of Phil. 1:6). It is the Holy Spirit who initiates, continues and completes this work in every believer. We must always rejoice in these truths and not react away from the true Biblical doctrine of the Holy Spirit.

(v) This book makes no claim to be an exhaustive treatment—others have presented very thorough historical and analytical studies which are quoted in the text. My aim is only to consider dispassionately what the Bible says in relation to the problem before us. I believe that having to think about this matter will become a blessing, because in turning afresh to the Word of God we shall realize more deeply the fullness of God's salvation in Jesus Christ His Son through the ministry of His Holy Spirit both in His Church and in our individual lives.

Singapore, December 1968

PART I: PETER

The Apostle Peter was a disciple of our Lord from the beginning. He heard all His teaching, companied with Him from the time of the baptism of John and was one of the witnesses of His resurrection. It was Peter who on the Day of Pentecost stood up with the eleven and preached the first great evangelistic sermon, concluding with the famous words, 'Repent, and be baptized every one of you in the name of Jesus Christ for the forgiveness of your sins; and you shall receive the gift of the Holy Spirit.' It was also Peter who was sent with John to Samaria and there 'prayed for them that they might receive the Holy Spirit . . . they laid their hands on them and they received the Holy Spirit'. And again, it was Peter who was so clearly guided in relation to the remarkable events involving Cornelius and his household and friends.

The Gospel of Mark is generally considered to represent the substance of the Apostle Peter's evangelistic teaching. In Acts a number of his sermons are recorded, and in addition we possess two letters written by him. We may expect, therefore, that this material will reflect Peter's teaching and his own personal experience with regard to the Holy Spirit and His gifts.

The New Testament material referring explicitly to 'speaking in tongues' is remarkably concentrated. Apart from one reference in the longer ending of Mark, it is confined to three references in the Acts of the Apostles and then within three chapters in the first letter to the Corinthians. Lest anyone jump to any hasty and unconsidered verdict on this, it is worth adding that apart from the references in the Gospels and Acts to the Lord's Supper, this, too, is mentioned only in Corinthians.

I. THE MARK REFERENCE

Mark 16:17, 18: '*And these signs will accompany those who believe; in my name they will cast out demons; they will speak*

*in new tongues; they will pick up serpents, and if they drink
any deadly thing, it will not hurt them; they will lay hands on
the sick; and they will recover.'*

Now in view of the great use made of this text as the *only*
dominical statement in relation to tongues, it is worth
while pointing out that this section is omitted in some
MSS. and stigmatized as spurious by some early authorities
such as Eusebius and Jerome. As an example of an early
tradition it may well be genuine, and is certainly primitive,
but it does not seem to belong to the actual text of the Gospel
as it stands. It is, therefore, extremely unwise to place too
much weight upon this reference. If one wished, of course,
to indulge in logical argumentation, the phrase 'they will
speak in new tongues' (v. 17) should be paralleled by the
phrase 'they will pick up serpents' (v. 18). Both these
statements are absolute and are not conditional as in the
phrase 'if they drink any deadly thing, it will not hurt
them' (v. 18). The words do not say *'if'* you pick up a
serpent it won't bite you, but 'they will do it'. In other
words, logically this verse could be used to prove that
Biblical Christians should not only be 'tongue speakers'
but also 'snake handlers'. We therefore need to be cautious
in using this section, selecting the one phrase to support our
argument while ignoring the rest, in view of its very doubt-
ful provenance.

II. THE ACTS REFERENCES

Speaking in tongues is only mentioned specifically on three
occasions in the Acts of the Apostles, although it may
reasonably be deduced (but not without the possibility of
disagreement) from the description of what took place in
Samaria. In view of all that is argued from these passages,
three preliminary comments about them need to be made:

(i) Many insist that these passages may be interpreted in
only one way: they *must* teach the 'baptism of the Spirit'
as a second experience. But what must be said is that we cannot go further than to say that they *may* teach this. It is a
possible interpretation, but not the sole one.

(ii) It is a principle of Bible interpretation that Biblical events may *illustrate* Biblical doctrine but they never in themselves *constitute* Biblical doctrine. In other words, it is dangerous to construct your doctrines out of events, because the latter are so often open to differing interpretations. It is wise to interpret Biblical events and narratives in the light of the established doctrine of Scripture. This is argued by John Stott with characteristic lucidity in his booklet, *The Baptism and Fullness of the Holy Spirit*, Inter-Varsity Press, page 6. But, in the booklet, *Baptized in One Spirit: the meaning of I Corinthians* 12:13 published by the Fountain Trust, John Baker makes a good case for some qualification of this general principle. He points out that the narrative passages of Scripture are also inspired and 'profitable for doctrine' and he reinforces this with a further five arguments. Baker makes his point and we must not therefore use this general principle of Biblical interpretation in such a way as to ignore the teaching of the Acts passages altogether! There may be, as we shall see, places where there are hints in the narrative passages themselves of the way in which they ought to be understood.

(iii) We must notice the contrast between the Acts events and the Corinthian practice of the gift of tongues. The occurrences in Acts are *all* an initial evidential phenomenon which fell unexpectedly and irresistibly upon *whole groups* of people: the 120, Cornelius and his kinsmen and close friends, and about twelve in Ephesus respectively—and in each case they *all* seem to have spoken *simultaneously*. In not one of these cases were those concerned actually seeking the gift of tongues, although in Acts 2 they *were* waiting for enduement with power by the Holy Spirit. In Corinthians, on the other hand, it is a *continuing* gift to individuals and one which they are expected to control, speaking one by one in turn, and not at all unless there is an interpreter. It is certainly arguable, therefore, that the events described in Acts and the practice described in Corinthians are definitely distinct. There is little unity of opinion on this particular matter even among the various Pentecostal groups. If the teaching in this connection is so obvious, why is it not equally obvious to all? And why should there be such variety of interpretation of the obvious? Some Pentecostals make a distinction between the initial evidential speaking in tongues and the regular practice of a specific 'gift of tongues', while others identify the two experiences.

We shall now consider each reference more fully.

I. Acts, chapter 2

Interpretation of this wonderful passage is related to three main questions: the composition of the group and the people involved, the nature of the 'tongues' involved and the significance of the event.

A. *The composition of the group and the people involved*

There were three main groups of people involved on the Day of Pentecost—the 120 disciples who spoke in tongues, those who mocked and seem therefore *not* to have understood what was said, and the multitude of 'dwellers in Jerusalem, Jews, devout men from every nation under heaven', who were amazed and wondered because they heard in their own tongues the mighty works of God.

The word 'Jews' is omitted in the Codex Sinaiticus, but 'devout men', which is included, is used in the New Testament *only* of Jews. So it is clear that these people were in fact Jews and proselytes (v. 10). It is sometimes suggested that the word for 'dwellers' means that these people were permanent residents in Jerusalem, but the more usual interpretation is that they were Jews and proselytes from the dispersion who had come to stay in Jerusalem for Pentecost.

B. *The nature of the 'tongues' involved*

The problem arises partly because all Jews from the west would understand Greek and all those from further off could understand Aramaic. Thus the outburst of foreign languages was not really necessary for communication. Evidence for this is found in the fact that Peter spoke to them all afterwards, not in 'tongues' but in normal speech, and apparently without the need for interpretation (v. 14). The Pentecostals agree that the initial 'tongues' were intelligible foreign languages. Some commentators insist that *all* 'tongues' are in fact languages, although unknown to people present. Others draw attention to the following contrasts between the 'tongues' of the Day of Pentecost and those at Corinth:

Pentecost	*Corinth*
In Jerusalem *all* 120 spoke in tongues.	At Corinth 'not all' spoke in tongues.
'Tongues' were understood by many, or most (Acts 2:7).	'Tongues' were understood by none, except the interpreter.
They were spoken to men (Acts 2:6).	They were spoken to God (1 Cor. 14:2).
No interpreter needed (Acts 2:8).	Forbidden unless interpreted (1 Cor. 14:28).
Brought salvation to others.	Edified only the speakers (1 Cor. 14:4).

There is therefore a very strong case for the view that the Pentecost event was *different* from the normal occurrence and practice of the gift of tongues as described in Corinth; at Pentecost it was intelligible without interpretation, whereas the normal gift of tongues is incomprehensible to the hearers. If this distinction is maintained it is embarrassing to those who wish to adopt an exclusively Pentecostal interpretation.

C. *The significance of the event*

Here we meet the fundamental problem. Is what happened on the day of Pentecost *typical* of what should happen whenever the Holy Spirit enters the hearts of men? Or is it something unusual, even unique, which has affected the whole Church—a once-for-all 'baptism of the Spirit' which cannot be repeated?

The general Pentecostal position is that *all* believers

should pass through a Pentecostal experience similar to that in Acts 2: that that experience was typical, is normative and should be the common experience of every believer.

Against this viewpoint it may be argued:

(i) *that several evidential signs occurred.*

Why select only tongues-speaking as the sign? Why not insist on the rushing wind or the tongues of fire?

(ii) *that only a comparatively small group spoke in tongues.*

It was the 120 disciples who had this wonderful experience and *not*, according to the record, the 3,000 who believed as a result of Peter's preaching.

(iii) *that there is only a slight connection between 'speaking in tongues' and being 'filled with the Spirit'.* Of nine references in Acts to being filled or being full of the Holy Spirit, this is the *only* occasion when being filled with the Spirit is directly connected with speaking in tongues.

(iv) *that the Pentecostal experience differed from the Corinthian practice.*

As argued above, the Pentecostal 'tongues' cannot be identified with the 'gift of tongues' described in Corinthians, although both are due to the inspiration of the Holy Spirit.

(v) *that Peter's testimony as to the significance of the Day of Pentecost does not support the 'Pentecostal' argument.* In Acts 11, vv. 15 and 16, when Peter is commenting upon what happened in the house of Cornelius, he says:

'As I began to speak, the Holy Spirit fell on them just as on us at the beginning. And I remembered the word of the Lord, how he said, "John baptized with water, but you shall be baptized with the Holy Spirit." If then God gave the same gift to them as he gave to us when we believed in the Lord Jesus Christ, who was I that I could withstand God?'

Now this passage is very interesting because it clearly identifies both what happened at Pentecost in Acts 2, *and* what happened in the house of Cornelius in Acts 11, with the 'baptism of the Holy Spirit' about which the Lord spoke and about which John the Baptist prophesied. It is also contrasted with John's baptism with water. But even *more* significant is the full force of Peter's words. If we are to accept a 'Pentecostal' position, we must believe that the coming of the Holy Spirit upon converts was a matter of *general* occurrence which would have been familiar to every Christian evangelist: certainly something which Peter himself would have observed over and over again. In the view of 'Pentecostals', every time Peter preached and called for men to believe and to be baptized, each time hands were laid on them the signs of the 'baptism' should have been seen over and over again. Pentecostals believe that the experience of the 120 disciples at Pentecost was *not* unique, except in so far as it was the first occasion on which this happened: subsequently believers on whom hands were laid would also receive 'the gift of the Holy Spirit'. The word 'of', understood as an objective genitive, is taken to mean that every believer received the Holy Spirit with sensible, discernible evidence in the form of speaking in tongues. But this is *not* what Peter says. What he says is that what happened in the house of Cornelius was the same thing that happened *to us* (that is, the Apostles and brethren gathered in Jerusalem) 'at the beginning'. And he reinforces it by saying, 'And I remembered the word of the Lord.' The whole force of these words is lost *entirely* if this was a general experience. There would be no point at all in making this remark if Acts 2 is to be understood as normal rather than special and if the initial falling of the Holy Spirit upon people was habitually evidenced by speaking in tongues.

(vi) *The actual significance of the Jewish annual commemoration of Pentecost.*

Another necessity in reaching an understanding of the significance of the day of Pentecost is to consider the origin and meaning of the Feast as celebrated by the Jews. The unique experience of the Passover deliverance from Egypt was followed fifty days later by the giving of the Law on Mount Sinai: this is the occasion which from the inter-

testamental period onward was commemorated at Pentecost. The fulfilment of the unique Passover deliverance was
in the unique event of Calvary. The New Testament fulfilment of the giving of the Law fifty days later was the giving
of the Spirit—an equally unique event. It is possible to
evade the force of this argument by insisting that the salvation made possible by the unique event of Calvary has to be
individually experienced subsequently: thus the unique
event of Pentecost must also be personally appropriated
one by one. But, in fact, it is not Calvary itself which is
repeated but rather the appropriation of its benefits.
Similarly, it is not the day of Pentecost which is to be
repeated but the appropriation of the benefits of that
once-for-all event.

The importance of what happened in Acts 2 lies in the
fact that it was a sign to Judaism in fulfilment of Joel's
prophecy; it confirmed the risen Christ to be the true
Messiah; and it emphasized the wider implication of an
exclusive Judaism being addressed for the first time by the
Lord Jehovah in the languages of the Gentiles. What then did
Peter mean when he said, 'Repent, and be baptized every
one of you in the name of Jesus Christ for the forgiveness
of your sins; and you shall receive the gift of the Holy
Spirit'? Does the 'gift of the Holy Spirit' mean a 'gift of
tongues'? Is 'of' an *objective* genitive, that is to say, a gift
which the Holy Spirit gives? Is it not rather, as seems probable, to be understood as a *subjective* genitive, that is to
say, not a gift given *by* the Holy Spirit so much as the gift
of the Holy Spirit Himself?' (see F. F. Bruce, *Acts: The
New London Commentary*, p. 77).

II. Acts, chapter 8

When Peter and John were sent by the Jerusalem Apostles
to the new converts in Samaria, they 'prayed for them that
they might receive the Holy Spirit; for it had not yet
fallen on any of them, but they had only been baptized in
the name of the Lord Jesus. Then they laid their hands on
them and they received the Holy Spirit. Now when Simon

saw that the Spirit was given through the laying on of the apostles' hands. . . .'

Although we are not told that the Samaritans did speak with tongues after the Apostles had laid hands on them, it is arguable that there must have been some sensible evidence of their having received the Spirit; it is possible, therefore, to interpret this event in a 'Pentecostal' sense as implying the possibility of two distinct experiences:

(i) that people may believe and be baptized in the name of Jesus, as happened in Samaria (v. 12).

(ii) that after a definite passage of time hands may be laid on them and then they in a special sense receive the Holy Spirit (vv. 15–17).

It is in this passage particularly that the problem of Biblical interpretation becomes acute. Whatever our views, how are we to understand the statement that baptized believers had 'not yet received the Holy Spirit'?

In the light of such clear statements as those in Ephesians 1:13, 'On believing you were sealed with the promised Holy Spirit,' or Romans 8:9 ff., 'Any one who does not have the Spirit of Christ does not belong to him,' how is it possible to say that genuine believers, and baptized believers to boot, had not yet received the Holy Spirit?

Should we interpret the rest of the New Testament in the light of this Samaritan event, especially when tongues-speaking is not specifically mentioned? Or should we interpret this admittedly very difficult passage in the light of the general New Testament teaching? Are we to take this difficult passage and make it the basis of a 'double experience' teaching or not? Obviously it could be so interpreted. It could equally be interpreted to mean that the Holy Spirit is given to all Anglicans through the laying on of the hands of the bishop in confirmation. But most of us would not wish to make such a deduction. Neither of these possible interpretations is one which we *must* espouse. And this surely is the point here—the passage does not bind us to a 'double experience' interpretation. Further points for consideration are:

B

(a) In Acts 2 people believed and were baptized, but there is no record of a subsequent laying on of hands or any suggestion that those who were baptized spoke in tongues.

(b) In Acts 10:44 we read that the Holy Spirit fell on people before there had been an expression of faith and without laying on of hands. In this case water baptism was *subsequent* to their experience of receiving the Holy Spirit (v. 47).

(c) There are many other places in the book of Acts where it is recorded that people came to genuine faith, but without any special manifestation of the Spirit apparently being bestowed. Hoekema (*What about Tongue-Speaking?*, Paternoster Press) lists them as follows (p. 80): 'The lame man is healed in (Acts) 3. Those who subsequently believed 4:4. Those who believed after the death of Ananias 5:14. The great company of priests 6:7. The Ethiopian eunuch 8:36. The many who believed in Joppa 9:42. Those who turned to the Lord in Syrian Antioch 11:21. The proconsul at Cyprus 13:12. The believers in Pisidian Antioch 13:43. The believers in Iconium 14:1. The disciples at Derbe 14:21. Lydia 16:14. The Philippian jailer 16:34. The believers in Thessalonica 17:4. The Bereans 17:11, 12ff. The Atheneans 17:34. Those in Corinth 18:4. Crispus and other Corinthians 18:8. Some of the Jews at Rome 28:24.' It is thus impossible to set this isolated Samaritan event against all these other events and argue that what took place in Samaria was the normal thing and typical of what happened whenever anyone in the Acts period became a Christian. The most that can be said about the Samaritan occurrence—and, we repeat, 'tongues' are not specifically mentioned—is that a 'double experience' is one possible interpretation. So also is the 'traditional' interpretation which recognizes how difficult it was for Jews to believe that the despised Samaritans, who used an emended Pentateuch and whose beliefs were heterodox, could possibly be included within the terms of the New Covenant. Therefore, just as Barnabas was later sent to Antioch by the Church at Jerusalem on a 'mission of enquiry' to discover whether approval could be given to what had happened there, so here the two leading

Apostles were sent from Jerusalem to investigate the remarkable events in Samaria. Had Philip, whose 'job description' had been that he should serve tables, perhaps exceeded his terms of reference? It therefore seems that the reception of Samaritans into the New Covenant Church (v. 12) now received the stamp of approval of two of the Apostles. Through them was given the manifest evidence of receiving the Holy Spirit comparable to the experience of the 120 on the Day of Pentecost. It may thus be interpreted as a sign given for the benefit of Judaistic Christians enabling them to accept the Samaritans as brethren.

Both of these views may equally be rejected as being no more than conjectural. Neither is clearly supportable from other passages of Scripture. But what is true of one is true of both.

III. Acts, chapter 10

In the house of Cornelius the Holy Spirit fell on all who heard the Word (v. 44) and the six circumcised believers with Peter were amazed that the gift of the Holy Spirit should be poured even on the Gentiles. 'For' (by way of explanation) 'they heard them speaking in tongues and extolling God' (v. 46). It is most pointed here that speaking in tongues seems to be interpreted by the historian specifically as the evidence to Jewish Christians that the Holy Spirit had indeed fallen upon Gentiles, and *unbaptized Gentiles* at that. It was evidence primarily to Peter and his companions. Subsequently it was evidence to the Jerusalem Church that God had accepted and cleansed the unclean Gentiles. This is clearly the interpretation of the event which the passage itself suggests: for the narrative assumes the impossibility of Jews believing that *Gentiles* could receive the Holy Spirit as well as themselves. Peter says, 'Well, they *have*! There's no mistaking it!' Without the 'tongues' sign it is possible that the Gentiles would not have been accepted as true Christians by the Jewish believers. Since Peter identifies what happened in the house of Cornelius with what happened 'in the beginning' in the experience of the 120, we *may* call the experience in the house of Cornelius the 'baptism with the Holy Spirit.'

Now how are we to interpret *this* event? Notice that if it is possible to use the Acts 8 narrative as an argument in favour of the necessity of a 'double experience' it is equally possible to adduce this passage in Acts 10 as evidence for the necessity of only a 'single experience'. Thus the danger of arguing from narratives is plain to see. Acts 8 can be used to prove that there have got to be two experiences. But Acts 10 can be used to prove that there must only be one and that the bestowal of the Holy Spirit was simultaneous with coming to faith. It is clearly consonant with our earlier understanding of the events in Acts 8 being a sign to the Jews of the reception of Samaritans, to interpret *this* passage as equally evidence to the Jews of the reception of Gentiles. This extension of the Acts 2 Pentecost experience was a clear and irrefutable demonstration that Gentiles could be saved and should be received into the Church without hesitation.

IV.   Acts, chapter 19

Peter was not present on this occasion, but the incident is included here as the fourth of the Acts passages referring to the Holy Spirit coming on believers and the third which specifically mentions 'speaking in tongues'. At Ephesus Paul finds a group of about twelve men who are described as 'disciples'. The point here is that when Paul asked his question of these men, he was under the impression that they were genuine disciples. It may be asked with some reason, 'Why then did he ask people whom he assumed to be Christians whether or not they had received the Holy Spirit, if it is axiomatic that all disciples on believing receive the Holy Spirit?' Thus runs the argument. My own obtuseness for many years in grasping this point arose because this narrative is frequently used in Japan, where I was a missionary, and elsewhere, as an argument in favour of a second 'sanctification' experience. These Ephesians are regarded as defective Christians who needed a second experience. One was always arguing, therefore, that these people weren't Christians at all! They were only the disciples of John. But the point of the 'Pentecostal' argument here must be grasped: namely, that Paul asked this question of men whom he *thought* were disciples. That is important. It is clearly stated that when Paul had laid his hands upon them the Holy Spirit came upon them (v. 6). This passage needs some unravelling. The problems are twofold:

(i) *Translation.* The wording of the Authorized Version, 'Have ye received the Holy Spirit since ye believed?' (v. 2) does seem to imply a second experience subsequent to initial saving faith. A quick glance at other versions of the Bible and various commentaries, however, will show that an accurate translation of the Greek should be 'Did you receive the Holy Spirit on believing?' (cf. F. F. Bruce, *The Acts of the Apostles*, Greek text commentary, p. 353: 'The *coincident aorist participle* is doctrinally important'). In questioning somebody with problems about assurance of salvation this is a question that one could quite easily ask, 'Did you receive the Holy Spirit when you believed?' And, of course, if he is a believer he ought to reply, 'Yes, of course I did!' (It is not unlike Paul's repetitive 'Know you not . . .?' to the Corinthians. 'Don't you know,' he says, 'that you are a temple of the Holy Spirit?'.)

(ii) *Interpretation.* It cannot be argued that this passage proves that every believer must receive Spirit baptism with speaking in tongues subsequent to his conversion. These twelve at Ephesus were not really converted to begin with. They had no saving faith in Christ and their first baptism was invalid. Again it can be argued that at Ephesus there were special circumstances, and that this instance was a sign to the disciples of John: a sign that they had done the proper thing in moving on from John's teaching to believing in Christ of whom John spoke, as 'One who will baptize you with the Holy Spirit'.

V. Summary of the Acts Evidence

The question to be decided is: Were these three or four events recorded because they were unusual, significant and in varying degrees *unique*? Or on the other hand because, far from being unique, they were to be regarded as *typical* of what happened time and time again, and a pattern of what ought to happen every time a person comes to a living experience of Christ?

The traditional view considers these events as marking decisive steps forward in the purpose of God and thus talks of the 'Samaritan' or 'Gentile' Pentecost. A slight modification of the traditional view sees these three or four occurrences of speaking in tongues as special signs to Judaistic Christianity (with respect both to the Gentiles and to the Samaritans) and to John's disciples respectively. It is surely significant that the author of the Acts does not record tongues as a result of evangelism on any of the many other occasions listed above. Attention is also called to the fact that though the expression 'filled with the Spirit' is used on a number of occasions in Acts, it is only in Acts 2 that the fullness of the Holy Spirit is connected with speaking in tongues.

It is important to remember that the 'Pentecostal' case for Spirit baptism stands or falls with the Acts material. Pentecostals readily admit that the Corinthian references give not the slightest hint that the charismatic gift of tongues is directly associated with an initial baptism with the Holy Spirit. It is impossible to prove from the Corinthian material that 'glossolalia' is the initial physical evidence of the baptism of the Spirit. If this can be proved at all from Scripture as distinct from experience it *has* to be proved from the book of Acts and, as we have seen, this is extremely difficult.

One realizes that this statement may seem critical of those who espouse the 'Pentecostal' position, but it must be honestly considered. One is *not* denying that theirs is a *possible* position to adopt but saying that it is not sufficiently *certain* to warrant dogmatism and so to endanger 'the unity of the Spirit'. Nor is there any basis, on the evidence of these passages alone, for relegating other baptized believers to an inferior status, because they have not had a clearly marked second experience, termed 'the baptism of the Spirit' and evidenced by speaking in tongues.

III. THE EVIDENCE OF THE EPISTLES

The Apostle Peter was one of the leading characters on three of the four significant occasions recorded by Luke in Acts. In view of this we can be quite certain that Peter at least was clear in his own mind what interpretation should be placed upon these events. He was *there*. If the doctrine of the 'baptism of the Spirit' is as crucial as advocates of the 'Pentecostal' position would make out, if it warrants emphasis and repetition above all other doctrines, then it is puzzling to know why it is not more clearly set out for us in Peter's own writings. In the Gospel of Mark there is the highly problematical longer ending, but there is not even a parallel to the Luke 11:13 phrase, 'How much more will the heavenly Father give the Holy Spirit to those who ask him?' Even when in Acts, chapter 2, Peter is explicitly explaining the remarkable event which has just occurred in the falling of the Holy Spirit upon the 120, he identifies the prophecy of Joel with the event which has just occurred without implying that it must subsequently be repeated over and over again. His sermon in Acts 3 includes no mention of the Holy Spirit at all.

But most significant of all are Peter's letters. Protagonists of a 'Pentecostal' position stress the doctrine of the Holy Spirit above all others. Sometimes they seem to have more to say about the Holy Spirit (albeit unintentionally) than about the Lord Jesus Himself. Now if this were the correct position we should surely expect that Peter of all people would set out this doctrine unmistakably. In his first letter, Peter declares that the elect are set apart by the Spirit for obedience to Jesus Christ and for sprinkling with His blood (1:2). He indicates the work of the Holy Spirit in prophets as they predicted the sufferings and the glory of Christ (1:11). (Compare the references to Christ and the references to the Holy Spirit.) Finally Peter turns to the subject of gifts (4:10) and says that gifts are received by each believer from God, that they are to be employed for one another, and that whoever speaks is to do it as one who 'utters oracles of God' (4:11). He refers not to some special and particular kind of ecstatic speaking, but to *all* Christian public speaking and urges that this is to be done in the power of the Spirit. (This is how we should also understand 1 Corinthians 1:5 'That in every way you were enriched in him with all speech and all knowledge . . .'.) These are the only references in Peter's first epistle to the Holy Spirit. It cannot honestly be claimed that Peter places any emphasis on a 'Pentecostal' interpretation of the Acts event as something of first importance. One needs of course to be cautious about arguments from silence but, as often as not, neo-Pentecostal arguments from Acts and the Epistles are arguments from silence! We are told, for example, that new converts always had the experience of being filled with the Spirit and speaking in tongues, but Acts does not say so specifically—it is merely assumed. We are aware of the familiar argument that Paul did not write about 'the baptism of the Holy Spirit' in Ephesians because the Ephesian Christians had already received 'the baptism' (cf. Acts 19). The bland assumption is made that the twelve former disciples of John were the only Ephesian Christians and that the general letter known to us as 'Ephesians' was addressed only to the Church in Ephesus. The arguments from silence are extensive! It seems equally fair to argue that, if this doctrine of Spirit baptism is as important and as fundamental as some would have us believe, Peter is strangely silent about it.

The above discussion, if it succeeds in bringing brethren to be of one mind by appreciating the strength of each other's viewpoints, is far from barren. But to be positive!

When Peter stood before the Sanhedrin we read that Peter was a man 'filled with the Holy Spirit' (Acts 4:8). What did this experience mean to Peter? It meant that he preached to the rulers that 'there is salvation in no one else, for there is no other name under heaven given among men by which we must be saved'. They saw the boldness of

Peter and John in preaching the Gospel—a thing that happens when people are filled with the Holy Spirit. The rulers perceived that they were uneducated and common men, and wondered. For Peter, therefore, the fullness of the Holy Spirit meant that he was able to speak with power; he was inspired by the Holy Spirit to speak the oracles of God with a boldness and an ability which transcended his own natural abilities and educational disadvantages.

The question therefore is: do we know this experience of Peter's of which Scripture speaks so unequivocally? Do we know the fullness of the Holy Spirit in our evangelistic preaching? Probably all of us in some measure would cry out from our hearts, 'Yes, I do know the Holy Spirit's help and enabling in preaching!' And this would be true whether we hold the 'Pentecostal' view of speaking in tongues or not. In fact, this experimental conviction is shared by those who have differing convictions with regard to speaking in tongues. This experience we *all* know in some measure. It hurts and grieves us when brethren knowing the undergirding of the Holy Spirit in their preaching find that other brethren appear to claim a monopoly of the Holy Spirit's operation. No one questions that for preaching we ought to seek habitually the inspiration of the Holy Spirit. Everyone must surely agree that we all need the power and enabling of the Holy Spirit always to speak as the oracles of God. We must not limit Spirit-inspired utterance to 'glossolalia' or special charismatic utterances limited to a few special Christians. This empowering with the Holy Spirit in utterance and for the proclamation of the Gospel involves the overcoming of our natural deficiencies, of which we are only too conscious. The prayer of my own heart as we think of Peter as a man filled with the Holy Spirit is that *all* of us, whatever the nature of our work, may seek and expect the power and enabling of the Holy Spirit so as to witness for Him with boldness. In Acts 4 we read, 'They were all filled with the Holy Spirit and spoke the word of God with boldness.' It is this speaking-in-evangelism and not speaking-in-tongues which is the *outstanding* lesson of a

study of what Peter says and what he experiences of the
Holy Spirit. On *one occasion* only is he said to have spoken
in tongues, but it is recorded that he *habitually* preached in
the power of the Holy Spirit; and he exhorts us to do the
same! (1 Pet. 4:11).

If you are going to seek some gift of the Holy Spirit for
your ministry, Peter would surely echo Paul's words to you,
'I would rather speak five words with my mind . . . than ten
thousand words in a tongue.' Is not this our longing—
to speak words which will be clearly understood by the un-
saved that will lead to their conversion? that every one of
us should know the power of the Holy Spirit enabling us to
preach the glorious Gospel effectively? The consideration
of Peter as a man filled with the Holy Spirit challenges us
to speak with the ability which God gives through His
Holy Spirit. What we most need is that same unity which
the disciples enjoyed in Acts, chapter 2: a unity which
issued in Gospel proclamation and a great harvest; a unity
such that, together with the converts, they were of one heart
and one soul and *together*, not divided, they went out to win
other people for our Lord Jesus Christ in the power of that
same Spirit.

Part II: PAUL

I. THE ACTS REFERENCES

None can doubt that Paul was a man filled with the Holy Spirit. We meet him first in Acts, chapter 9, where we find Ananias laying hands on him and saying: ' "Brother Saul, the Lord Jesus who appeared to you on the road by which you came, hath sent me that you may regain your sight and be *filled with the Holy Spirit*." And immediately something like scales fell from his eyes and he regained his sight. Then he rose and was baptized, and took food and was strengthened' (Acts 9:17–19). Paul was filled with the Holy Spirit at that moment, but there is no indication in the text that he then spoke in tongues. It is a gratuitous and irresponsible use of the Bible to maintain that he did. In Acts 13:9 he is again described as 'filled with the Holy Spirit' when he rebuked Elymas the sorcerer. The third reference in the Acts to Paul and the Holy Spirit is in Acts 19 when Paul first questioned, re-baptized and laid hands on the twelve disciples of John in Ephesus who then 'spoke with tongues and prophesied' (see Part I).

II. THE EPISTLES REFERENCES

We have no less than eighty-seven chapters of the Epistles from the hand of Paul. If he wrote Hebrews that would make it a good round hundred. But of all Paul's writings only three chapters treat our subject specifically. Moreover, we shall need to examine Paul's teaching on this matter in the light of his other writings wherever they have some bearing upon it.

I. 1 Corinthians, chapters 12–14

In these Corinthian chapters Paul is concerned with two main problems relating to tongues. Firstly, the danger of a *counterfeit* of the gift, and secondly, the danger of *abuse* of the gift, albeit a genuine gift. There is a possibility that the genuine gift may be misused: the gift is not self-controlling and must therefore be disciplined and restrained. Two other gifts of the Spirit are therefore available to ensure that the Church is not either led into error by a *spurious* gift or thrown into confusion by an *undisciplined* gift. In the list of nine gifts (12:8–10) the juxtaposition of the last three gifts is extremely interesting and significant. The gift of tongues is sandwiched between two other gifts which are to control and moderate it—i.e. discernment of spirits and interpretation. The first of the three is to determine the origin of the 'tongues', while the third governs their content. This is a wonderful illustration of the perfect balance of the Word of God.

A. *The danger of counterfeits—the gift is not self-authenticating*

In 1 Corinthians 12, Paul comes to the subject of spiritual gifts. What he actually says is, 'Now concerning the pneumatikōn'. The translators omitted the article and inserted the word 'gifts' to make sense. The Greek word is used sometimes of things and sometimes of persons, so the phrase could very well be translated as 'Now concerning the *inspired*' (i.e. persons), and this fits well with the context. The point made by Paul is that people speaking under inspiration may be divided into those who are speaking by the Spirit of God and those who, while certainly inspired, are *not* speaking by the Spirit of God. The test that he gives cannot be applied to all spiritual gifts, some of which are gifts of action, but only to gifts of inspired words. Now previously the Corinthians had already been familiar as idol-worshippers with inspired persons, with oracles, speaking under the influence of false gods and moved by demonic influences (v. 2). But even now, converted and in the church, there is still a danger that a spirit other than the Spirit of God will speak through someone in the congregation. This aspect of the subject is, oddly enough, sometimes not discussed at all in 'Pentecostal' literature. No reflection is implied on a genuine gift by asserting with Scripture that there are also spurious gifts. This is what Paul asserts at the very beginning of his discussion of the subject, and the order of the gifts explains why he does so.

The mere occurrence of ecstatic utterance is not necessarily evidence of the work of the Holy Spirit. In apostolic times other criteria were needed. They are no less necessary today. But it would be quite ingenuous to generalize, because some particular manifestation is manifestly spurious, that therefore *all* speaking with tongues in *all* 'Pentecostal' gatherings is spurious and of the Devil. Like prayer and hymn-singing, 'glossolalia' is a widespread phenomenon. (Perhaps it is better to use this term of spurious manifestations and to use the word 'experience' for genuine ones.) 'Glossolalia' is a widespread phenomenon also found in Islam, Hinduism, Mormonism, spiritism, Voodoo and was associated with the mass hysterical phenomena of the Middle Ages known as 'dancing madness'. Clearly there is not only a genuine but also a spurious speaking in tongues. We may expect to find alongside the genuine, the Devil's counterfeit. We are used to counterfeit and true Christians. There is every reason also from Scripture to expect counterfeit tongues and counterfeit miracles. The whole discussion is often bedevilled—and that seems a suitable word—by the discussion of Pentecostalism in all its expressions or the current tongues movement in every instance as though it were a homogeneous mass—wholly good or wholly bad. Some point to counterfeits or excesses and want to write off the whole thing, while others point to apparently genuine and Holy Spirit inspired manifestations of tongues and want a kind of 'package deal' endorsement of the whole movement. Neither of these approaches is Biblically correct. We need this gift of discernment of spirits, for today no less than in apostolic times we may expect to find the Devil infiltrating the true with the false, raiding the fold in sheep's clothing, disguising himself as an angel of light and seeking to deceive the very elect. Now it is naturally hurtful to speak of spurious gifts among those who claim a genuine experience, but it must be emphasized that the gift is not self-authenticating. The individuals themselves may very well not *know* whether the gift which they have is a real or genuine gift; it therefore implies no quenching of the Spirit and no lack of charity to ask the questions which Scripture itself says ought to be asked.

Spurious examples of tongue-speaking are not all necessarily due to the work of demons or evil spirits. Some Christians think of speaking in tongues as a purely human phenomenon akin to automatic writing, trances and the like. It *is* possible to misconstrue manifestations of one's own deep unconsciousness as visitations of ultimate reality.

'Some recent experiments in the field of euphoric states of mind have shown us that practically all mystical experience can be produced through artificial means,' says Dr. Akbar Abdul-Haqq (Congress on Evangelism paper 'Theology of Evangelism', p. 6). Hoekema (*What about Tongue-Speaking?*, pp. 128–134) makes quotations from various sources which support this hypothesis.

It has been suggested that tongues-speaking as we observe it today is 'not of divine origin' but is the result of 'auto-suggestion, self-induced; piously, yes, but wrongly and unscripturally' (Robert Lindberg, *Presbyterian Guardian*, volume 34, No. 2, February 1965, p. 22).

But one thing may lead to another, as suggested by Jessie Penn Lewis: 'The repetition of a word many times seems to "detach" the tongue from the volitional use of it by the owner and place it at the disposal of the evil spirit as the wheel of an engine driven by petrol power. The repetition of words, therefore, apart from the deliberate volition of the person behind each word is dangerously liable to become like the "incantation" used by witch doctors in heathen lands and to have the same result, i.e. open the body to the working of the spirits' ('Spiritual Perils of To-day', *The Overcomer*, July 1965, p. 42).

Enough has been said to make it clear that all of us, whatever our viewpoint, should avoid sweeping generalizations. We should certainly not automatically assume that every occurrence of speaking in tongues is spurious or of the Devil. That speaking in tongues may be a genuine gift of the Holy Spirit is plainly taught here in these chapters in Corinthians. At the same time we must not with equal gullibility be led into affirming that because there is speaking in tongues, this must in every case be due to the ministry of the Holy Spirit Himself. This would be dangerous. Because the gift is *not* self-authenticating, in 1 Corinthians 12:3 we are clearly warned to apply certain tests; it is therefore in accord with Scripture and not in any sense quenching the Spirit or tempting the Spirit to put the test of asking whether the spirit will confess that 'Jesus is Lord'. There is the further test given to us by the Apostle John (1 John 4:1): 'Beloved, do not believe every spirit, but *test the spirits* to see whether they are of God; for many false prophets have gone out into the world. By this you know the Spirit of God: every spirit which confesses that Jesus Christ has come in the flesh is of God, and every spirit which does not confess Jesus is not of God. This is the spirit of anti-christ. . . .'

B. *The danger of misuse—the gift is not self-controlling*

From the twelfth verse of chapter 12, Paul uses the analogy of the body which consists of different organs exercising complementary functions and at the same time mutually interdependent. No part can exist independently of the other parts and each part needs the others in order to function properly itself. So Paul stresses that there are varieties of gifts (the word is now 'charismatōn' v. 4); that is, to one is given through the Spirit the utterance of wisdom (v. 8)—and how we need that gift!—and to another the utterance of knowledge (v. 8); to another faith, to another gifts of healing (v. 9); to another various kinds of tongues, etc. All of these (v. 11) are inspired by one and the same Spirit who apportions to each one individually as He wills.

It is difficult to see how, after reading these verses, it is possible to affirm that to *everyone* should be given 'various kinds of tongues'. The whole point of the passage which

follows is that different parts of the body have different
functions. All do *not* have the same function. All cannot do
the same thing. It is noteworthy that nowhere in this whole
section is there any direct statement associating speaking
in tongues with being filled with the Spirit. Paul is merely
describing the variety of gifts which are given for mutual
benefit. The chapter closes with the questions, 'Are all
apostles? Are all prophets? Are all teachers? Do all work
miracles? Do all possess gifts of healing? Do all speak with
tongues? Do all interpret?' (vv. 29 and 30). Surely these
questions are sufficient to make it clear that the gifts
mentioned were *not* common to every member of the Corinthian Church. The questions in the Greek are all introduced
with the particle *me* indicating that the answer 'no' is
expected.

It is not uncommon to hear an evasion of the force of the
above argument by suggesting that while not all possess the
public gift, all may in fact use it *privately*! Is this, we must
ask, an honest exposition of the passage? Certainly we may
understand the passage to mean that not all possess the
public gift of miracles or of teaching or of prophecy. But one
could scarcely argue that the gifts of miracles, teaching and
prophecy may still be exercised privately! To expound the
passage in this way makes nonsense of the plain meaning of
the text. The plain meaning of the passage is that only some
people exercise these gifts at all, not that all may exercise
them privately, if not publicly. Therefore, to assert, as
some do, that 'Everybody who has been baptized in the
Holy Spirit may and can speak in tongues if he desires to
do so' is plainly anti-Scriptural.

This being so, it becomes clear that even a genuine
gift of the Spirit may be misused in various ways. And
the passage indicates *three spiritual dangers* of possessing
a gift:

(i) *spiritual pride*. The danger indicated here is that
certain members may affirm that they do not need other
members. Paul clearly regards this as a mistake. The passage is a rebuke against any assumed sense of superiority.

Nobody is superior to others because of the gifts which God has sovereignly given (v. 11). All members need all other members and there is no place for spiritual pride over one's particular gift.

(ii) *disunity*. The second spiritual danger (v. 25) is that there may be *discord* in the body. 'A problem always arises when individual spiritual experiences disrupt or disdain the unity of the fellowship of the Church. All too frequently what are conceived of as advanced attainments in spiritual experience create divisions within groups of believers. Rather than being of mutual profit they become a source of party spirit and spiritual pride. All the gifts of the Spirit are given within the unity and for the edifying of the body; their effect is the test of their validity,' writes Jack F. Shepherd (editorial in *The Alliance Witness*, 3 March 1965). The point here surely is that the whole purpose of spiritual gifts is the edification and the strengthening of the body. A spiritual gift which divides the body is a contradiction in terms. It is questionable whether those who are divisive in this way can be regarded as really spiritual.

(iii) *lack of love* (ch. 13). 'If I speak in the tongues of men and of angels, but have not love, I am a noisy gong and a clanging cymbal.' This famous passage is often read right out of context. The context is, of course, the possession and use of spiritual gifts and Paul begins with the reference to 'tongues of men and of angels'. However richly we may be endowed with spiritual gifts, they are made void if we are lacking in the first and all-inclusive *fruit* of the Spirit—love (Galatians 5:23). There is a real spiritual danger in the possession of any gift, including tongues, that we may become proud and puffed up, contentious and divisive. Love is the wavelength which must be used if gifts are to communicate effectively the blessing of God.

Before continuing with a consideration of the practical dangers attending the use of the gift, we must digress slightly to discuss two other points of interpretation which arise in these chapters.

c

(a) *The meaning of 1 Corinthians 12: 13*

This is discussed in *The Baptism and Fullness of the Holy Spirit* by John Stott. Stott's interpretation is answered by John Baker in his booklet on the meaning of this verse (*Baptised in One Spirit: the meaning of 1 Corinthians* 12:13). Stott argues that 'the baptism of the Spirit' is mentioned in Scripture on seven specific occasions—John the Baptist's prophecy in the Gospels four times, our Lord's quotation of it in Acts 1:5, Peter's quotation of it in Acts 11 and the verse in question. He maintains that it is unwarrantable to make Jesus Christ the baptizer in six instances and the Holy Spirit the baptizer in the seventh. Therefore, it is through the Holy Spirit that we were baptized into Christ. The contrary position maintains that the Holy Spirit has indeed baptized us into the Body of Christ, but that it does not necessarily follow that Christ has baptized us all with the Holy Spirit. Stott uses this verse to establish that we *all* have *already* shared in this one baptism of the Spirit. It is 'a universal blessing for members of the covenant, because it is an initial blessing' (p. 19). *All* Christians, he argues, have already experienced the 'baptism of the Spirit'. Baker takes issue with Stott on this point and his argument is both tortuous and tedious! In fact, Baker is only out to prove that Stott's interpretation is 'not the only possible understanding or meaning of the verse' (p. 18). If one allows (and this is questionable) that he succeeds in doing this, it means that we are faced with two possible interpretations of the verse, though neither position hangs on this verse alone.

One wonders whether either a position which regards the baptism of the Spirit as completed past, or one which regards it as a desirable future experience is true to Scripture. This seems a very poverty-stricken exposition of the meaning of 'the baptism of the Spirit'. Our Lord taught (John 7:37–39) that the Spirit, when He is given, will well up in us like a bubbling spring to everlasting life (cf. John 4:14). Scripture also teaches that God has '*flooded* your hearts through His Spirit which is given to us' (Rom. 5:5). If, therefore, we think of a fountain which is overflowing in such a way that it is constantly immersed you have a better notion of what 'the baptism of the Spirit' ought to mean. It is not merely a past experience but rather an ever-fresh experience of constant total immersion![1]

As stated above 'the baptism of the Spirit' is referred to seven times in the New Testament. We must be careful lest we first adduce from experience what we mean by this phrase and then proceed to read this meaning into every reference. Rather we should examine the references first, note what they say, and then see how Scripture applies them. We have already observed that Peter refers 'the baptism of the Spirit' back to Pentecost and also identifies what happened in the house of Cornelius with Pentecost.

(b) *The Reformed view*

This was expounded by B. B. Warfield in a book first published as *Counterfeit Miracles* (Scribner, 1948). A later edition had the slightly less dogmatic and more charitable title of *Miracles Yesterday and Today* (Eerdmans, 1953). Recently this work was reprinted as a paperback (1965). This position is based not upon any clear statements of Scripture but on a series of reasonable deductions from Scripture. In the passage we are considering, he refers the failing of prophecy and speaking in tongues (1 Cor. 13:8) not to the final consummation but to the passing of the Church's period of immaturity before the full revelation provided by the writing of the New Testament. With reference to the letter to the Ephesians with its, chronologically, latest list of gifts, Warfield points out that the miracle gifts are entirely omitted. He argues, therefore, that the gifts were no longer required and that they belonged to a period of immaturity, of childish speaking which was to give way to maturity. There seems little evidence for such gifts between the apostolic age and the fourth century, so that Chrysostom (A.D. 345–407), when commenting on these very verses, could write,

[1] I am grateful to Rev. J. Tootill for this helpful thought.

'The whole passage is exceedingly obscure and the obscurity is occasioned by ignorance of facts and the cessation of happenings which were common in those days but unexampled in our own.'

We are reminded that Chrysostom was writing from Constantinople and an eastern church. Again, Augustine (A.D. 354–430) can write,

'That thing was done and it passed away. In the laying on of hands now that persons may receive the Holy Ghost, do we look that they should speak with tongues? Or when we laid the hands on these neophytes' (it is not clear whether he means infants or new converts) 'did each one of you look to see whether they would speak with tongues, and when he saw that they did not speak with tongues, were any of you so wrong minded as to say, these have not received the Holy Ghost, for had they received they would speak with tongues as was the case in those times?' (*Homilies on the First Epistle of John*, VI. 10, the seventh volume of the 'Nicene and post-Nicene fathers'). It is possible, Warfield says, to find 'glossolalia' exhibited by the Montanists and among the Gnostics, but it does seem to have died out very early in the main stream of Christian orthodoxy.

From Warfield's point of view, therefore, all modern claims to speaking in tongues must be spurious, a dangerous combination of jargon and psychopathology, found only in the lunatic fringe of Christendom and possibly inspired by the Devil. The argument is interesting, but even if you allow the withdrawal of the miracle gifts for many centuries, this is susceptible to the rejoinder that now a new period of church history is beginning in which the Lord is restoring these gifts to the Church as we approach the end time. And such a view could be supported from the Old Testament. Although the patriarchs did not perform miracles, there was suddenly an outburst of miraculous gifts during the time of Moses and Joshua. Such gifts then ceased for a sustained period and neither David nor Solomon performed miracles. But there is a further period of miraculous intervention in the times of Elijah and Elisha, after which these gifts cease until the time of Christ. The Warfield theory is ingenious, and dogmatically convenient, but we have to return the verdict of 'not proven'.

One interesting feature of Warfield's book is the chapter on 'Irvingite gifts'. In view of the tendency of some 'Pentecostal' writers to quote the Irvingites with approval as an example of a genuine occurrence of the gift of tongues, it is worth while referring to this exposure; in *As at the Beginning* (p. 21) Michael Harper recognizes this.

The Bible, we claim, is our guide in all matters of faith and conduct. The existence and use of a genuine gift *is* undoubtedly described in Scripture, although not, in my view, as an experience inseparable from the so-called 'baptism of the Holy Spirit', subsequent to conversion. If the Scripture is our guide, and if we cannot follow Warfield, then we have to recognize that there is such a thing as a genuine gift of tongues.

C. *Practical dangers attending the use of the gift*

The Church at Corinth had been experiencing disorder in public worship and Paul, while pronouncing that the exercise of the gift of tongues was not to be forbidden, insists that it must be very rigidly controlled. He explains this by saying that the first thing about a 'tongue' is that it is spoken to God (I Cor. 14-2); for it is unintelligible to the hearers (vv. 2, 9); and while a 'tongue' may edify the individual concerned (v. 4), it does not edify the church (vv. 3–5); unless the 'tongue' is interpreted, those with the gift must remain silent and not disturb the worship of others (vv. 5, 28); moreover speaking in tongues must be restricted to two individuals, at most three in any one meeting, and they must not all speak at once, but in turn and each 'tongue' is to be followed by interpretation (v. 27).

Another interesting point to be noted is the much discussed matter of women keeping silent in the churches (v. 34). The phrase 'to keep silent' is used (v. 28) when there is no interpreter and again (v. 30) when another is speaking. It would seem, therefore, in this context that a possible explanation of this much debated verse is that Paul is placing a further important limitation upon the use of tongues: no tongues unless by interpretation: not more than two or three in one meeting: and not at all by women! Certainly the preceding context of this verse would suggest that it should be understood specifically in the context of 'tongues'. The succeeding context, however, does not necessarily substantiate this. Nevertheless, this consideration may well give us reason to pause in view of the very considerable involvement of women in the 'glossolalia' movement.

D. *The use of the mind*

Although the mind is not consciously used when speaking in tongues (vv. 14, 15, 19), the use of the gift is still clearly under the control of individuals so that they can be expected to speak in turn, and keep silence if there is no interpreter (vv. 27–32). F. W. Robertson comments rather wonderfully, 'The Holy Ghost may mingle with man in three ways—with his body, and then you have what is called miracles; with his spirit, and then you have that exalted feeling which finds vent in what is called "tongues"; or with his intellect, and then you have prophecy.' Paul's suggestion to his hearers is that the gift of prophecy, though perhaps less spectacular and novel, is preferable for the edifying of the church as a whole (v. 5). But what is meant by the 'gift of prophecy'?

E. *The meaning of prophecy*

It is apparent from this passage that 'prophecy' refers to the commonest and most edifying type of speaking in the assembly. This indeed has been the traditional evangelical understanding. It is difficult to reconcile Paul's emphasis and stress upon 'prophecy' with the tendency of some to restrict its meaning to predictive prophecy. The New Testament has room for such predictive prophecy (Acts 11:28, 21:11) and it may be found also in 1 Corinthians 14:26 as 'a revelation'. It is hard however, to see, on such an understanding, how a New Testament gathering of Christians could find their time fully taken up with 'predictive' prophecy; one may question whether such a meeting would even be edifying. The New Testament usage conforms far more to the Old Testament usage of a fearless proclamation of the Word of God expounded in the light of the contemporary situation.

F. *The meaning of* 14:5
'Now I want you all to speak in tongues. . . .'

This verse has often been used to prove that all Christians ought to speak in tongues. Certainly, taken at its face value it seems quite clear that Paul is expressing a desire that tongues-speaking should be universal among the Corinthian Christians! But to take just part of a verse in this way leaves one open to at least a sneaking suspicion that one is not really doing justice to Paul's argument in the passage as a whole! It is helpful to take as a parallel what Paul says in 1 Corinthians 7:7 when he says that 'I would all men were even as I myself' (Authorized Version). It is equally possible to argue from this passage that Paul wished all Christians to be celibate and unmarried. The context makes it clear that this is not the case as he has already enunciated the general principle, 'Each man should have his own wife and each woman her own husband' (v. 2). The real force of 1 Corinthians 14:5 is, therefore, 'Now of course it would be very nice if all of you did speak in tongues! But far more than this what I want is that every one of you might prophesy.' It is therefore unwise to quote only a part of this verse without giving full weight to this particular Pauline mode of expression.

G. *Seeking spiritual gifts*
Another matter which requires consideration is that of 'seeking' spiritual gifts.[1] Like the other Epistles, these chapters of Corinthians are addressed not so much to individuals as to churches. This fact is often somewhat

[1] This point has been very helpfully made by the Rev. David Stewart of the New Zealand Bible Training Institute.

obscured for the English reader in that the second person singular and the plural 'you' are identical. Thus 'Earnestly desire the higher gifts' (12:31) and 'Make love your aim, and earnestly desire the spiritual things (pneumatika), especially that you may prophesy' (14:1) are not so much exhortations that I as an individual should seek an outstanding spiritual gift for myself (which may only be a rather unspiritual desire for pre-eminence) but rather that *we* should seek spiritual gifts for *us*! It suggests that, rather than an individualistic seeking for *personal* blessing, we should seek the Lord for spiritual gifts for our *congregation*. This is in accord with the teaching of chapter 12 about the varieties of gifts distributed at the sovereign will of the Spirit (12:11) and the glorious variety and division of functions within the body. There is nothing amiss in an earnest desire to be useful to the Lord, but in this context one can see how even more appropriate is the desire that all members of the body, each with different gifts and functions, should work together for His glory in the local congregation. This consideration should be modified in that individuals who possess the gift of tongues are told to pray for the complementary gift of interpretation (14:13). Rather than congratulating himself on having 'arrived' he should realize that he needs the other gift in order to perfect what he already has. Above all, he should get over the childish preference for novelty and excitement, not being a child in understanding (14:20), making love his aim and earnestly desiring the spiritual things (14:1).

However, prophecy is a gift especially to be desired for the fellowship (14:1). This is not because Paul himself does not possess the gift of tongues, for he says, 'I thank God that I speak in tongues more than you all' (v. 18). But in the congregation he would rather give five words with his mind than ten thousand in a tongue (v. 19). While this is certainly hyperbole, it indicates Paul's thinking on the matter.

The private use of tongues

How can we reconcile Paul's statement that he would rather

speak five words with his mind than ten thousand in a tongue with his giving thanks that he speaks in tongues more than all of them (v. 18)?[1] Possibly he means that he also possesses the ability to interpret and therefore, though he speaks in tongues, it is permissible for him to speak publicly and to give the interpretation to the church. If there is no interpretation Paul pronounces that one must keep silence in church and 'speak to himself and to God'.

What is implied by the words, 'Let each of them keep silence in the church and speak to himself and to God' (14:28)? Does it mean that the use of tongues is a form of prayer which may equally be silent or spoken out loud? Or does it mean that the use of tongues should be confined to private devotions? It is this private use of tongues which is currently stressed in the charismatic movement, although I have known people who have used tongues privately in their devotions years before this present emphasis. Certainly the possibility of using tongues privately is one way of reconciling Paul's apparently contradictory statements for which the traditional evangelical view seems to have no coherent explanation. Experimentally, a personal and private use of tongues has been claimed by many to have been of great spiritual and personal benefit. But this is an argument from experience rather than Scripture. The actual Scriptural warrant for 'solitary' speaking in tongues is not extensive. There is no example of it at all in the Acts narrative passages, and it is only understood by inference from the Corinthian passages. It could be urged, however, that in these chapters Paul is dealing largely with the public use and not with the private exercise of the gift of tongues. Private use raises the additional problem that it is not susceptible to the Biblical test of genuineness in the way that public exercise may be. The individual is not able to apply these tests to himself when he is 'inspired'. Presumably the test must then be in terms of the fruit of the Spirit and the long-term spiritual blessing attributable to the deepened prayer life.

[1] Some suggest it means that he spoke more foreign languages than any of them.

A further problem arises regarding the nature of tongues as a form of prayer. Some Christians have questioned whether prayer in which the mind is not used ought properly to be termed a 'higher' form of prayer than that which is rational and in which the mind is fully engaged in worshipping God. If we are to love the Lord our God not only with all our hearts and with all our spirits and also with all our minds, how can what is unintelligible be a higher form of prayer than that which is rational? A possible answer from the testimony of some friends is that through speaking in tongues in private devotions they are raised to a higher level of praise and worship, and having once reached this level of worship and adoration they are then able to begin praying intelligibly at the same level using the conscious mind. This would seem a possible valid answer to the objection. At the same time one must note cautiously that this doctrine of the private use of tongues is derived far more from the actual experience of individuals than from the direct mandate of Scripture.

II.   Romans, chapter 8

The eighth chapter of Romans has much to say about the work of the Holy Spirit. Verses 9–11 are a clear statement about the indwelling of the Holy Spirit in every believer. The person who does not have the Spirit of Christ 'does not belong to him'. A Christian is thus defined as being one who is indwelt by the Spirit of Christ—a basic Christian understanding which cannot be disregarded. It rules out the anomaly of a 'Christian' who has 'not received the Holy Spirit'. Verses 28–30 speak of God's tremendous purpose for every believer; they make it clear that those who are effectually called (this is the Spirit's ministry) 'he also justified; and those whom he justified he also glorified'. If it were true that a 'baptism of the Spirit' with tongues as a second experience is the norm for every believer, it is remarkable that the Holy Spirit apparently fails to bring the majority of Bible-believing Christians to this 'necessary' experience. Moreover, for long periods of church history, outstanding reformers, martyrs, and leaders of evangelical revivals, used to bring thousands into the Kingdom of God, neither experienced nor needed such a 'baptism'. Recognizing that God is sovereign in giving gifts to each one 'as He wills', why has He not then willed to give the gift of tongues if this is normal and necessary as some allege? How are we to understand verses like: 'All who are led by the Spirit of God are sons of God' (v. 14); 'When we cry, Abba! Father! it is the Spirit himself bearing witness with our spirit that we are children of God' (vv. 15, 16); 'We ourselves, who have the first fruits of the Spirit, groan inwardly' (v. 23); 'The Spirit helps us in our weakness; for we do not know how to pray as we ought, but the Spirit himself intercedes for us with sighs too deep for words' (v. 26)—do these verses apply, as we have always thought, to every born again believer? This would seem the most natural understanding. Are we justified in limiting them only to a small group of people within the Christian community who claim this special experience? Are we justified on the evidence in applying such verses as these to the few rather than to the many? Verse 26 could certainly be used to authenticate the personal use of tongues in prayer, but such an interpretation is only possible and not essential.

III. The Epistle to the Ephesians

This Epistle contains a remarkable number of references to the Holy Spirit. Because the Holy Spirit is the architect of the unity of the Christian temple (2:21–22) we have a corresponding responsibility to maintain the unity of the Spirit (4:3). The whole purpose of the gifts is to build up and strengthen the body: 'The whole body, joined and knit together by every joint with which it is supplied, when each part is working properly, makes bodily growth and upbuilds itself in love' (4:16). One is highly suspicious of trends or tendencies which lead to division. There is a dilemma for those who arrange meetings which are held, even if not explicitly, at least in the minds of those who organize them, for the purpose of propagating a particular teaching with regard to the 'baptism of the Spirit'. It is difficult to see how such meetings can take place without being open to the charge of divisiveness. There is no Scriptural warrant whatever for holding meetings with the specific intention of promoting the gift of tongues. In the Acts of the Apostles, those who spoke with tongues were never expecting or seeking the experience of speaking in tongues. It runs counter to Paul's whole argument in the Corinthian chapters to have special meetings in order to propagate speaking in tongues.

In this same general area, Ephesians 6:18, 'Pray at all times in the Spirit', is sometimes assumed to refer to 'praying for tongues'. But it is quite gratuitous to *assume* the meaning that one wishes to maintain! Like Christian speaking, all Christian praying should also be 'in the Spirit', since it is the Holy Spirit Himself who gives access to God in prayer (2:18).

IV. The Epistle to the Colossians

The problem with which Paul had to contend in the Colossian Church was a 'gnostic' view in which it was taught that the fullness of Christian truth was only to be known by a small group of initiates who possessed the 'epignosis', or full knowledge. It is against this factional group that Paul teaches emphatically that his desire is to teach '*every man* in *all* wisdom, that we may present *every man* mature in Christ' (1:28). His desire was that they may 'have all the riches of assured understanding' (2:2). Some people become so confused over this matter of speaking in tongues that they do not know what they really believe. Is it not wonderful that Paul shows that we may have 'all the riches of assured understanding, and the knowledge of God's mystery, of Christ, in whom are hid all the treasures of wisdom and knowledge. I say this in order that no one may delude you with beguiling speech' (2:2–4)? The Apostle continues: 'As therefore you received Christ Jesus the Lord, so live in him' (2:6), thus indicating that an assured understanding and all wisdom and knowledge are available to any and to all who have received Christ Jesus the Lord. Paul is eager to

stress that divisive groupings and sectarian cliques cannot
be tolerated within the Christian Church: 'Here there cannot
be Greek and Jew, circumcised and uncircumcised, barbarian,
Scythian, slave, free man, but Christ is all, and in all'
(3:11). If Christ is all and in every believer then all His
riches are available to all. Christians—and Christian leaders
in particular—need to be extremely careful lest they ever,
albeit unwittingly, espouse a kind of 'Christian gnosticism'
in which a select coterie is thought of as being in possession
of deeper truths and experience than others.

When exclusive teaching of this nature is given there will
always be those who are stumbled when they earnestly
seek 'the gift', but do not receive it. Dr. A. B. Simpson of
the Christian and Missionary Alliance, in his Annual Report
of 1907–8, wrote: 'One of the greatest errors is a disposition
to make special manifestations an evidence of the baptism
of the Holy Ghost, giving to them the name of Pentecost,
as though none had received the Spirit of Pentecost but
those who had the power to speak in tongues; thus leading
many sincere Christians to cast away their confidence,
and plunging them into the perplexity and darkness of
seeking after special manifestations other than God Himself.'
This solemn warning should be taken most seriously.

III. CONCLUSION FROM PAUL'S WRITINGS

In his Epistles Paul sets before us the wonders of God's
Salvation and all the riches that are ours in Christ, made
available to us through His Holy Spirit. It is impossible to
take the teaching of Paul as a whole and construct out of it
something sectarian or divisive. On the contrary, all believers are urged to avail themselves of everything that God
offers. How glorious is the full salvation which Christ has
given to us! 'How shall he not with him also freely give us
all things?' (Rom. 8:32, *AV*). Our Father is in heaven. Our
Saviour is now glorified in heaven and ever lives to make
intercession on our behalf. But the Holy Spirit is given to
every believer here on earth as a guarantee and pledge that
we shall be safely brought to our heavenly harbour. We are

assured of this despite all the difficulties we may meet on the way, through His guidance and leading, through His sovereign working in our hearts and lives 'to will and to do of (God's) good pleasure'. The Holy Spirit is the Great Pilot sent out from heaven specifically to steer us safely through the shoals and sandbanks, despite the cross-winds of doctrine, and to bring us safely to our desired haven. Because we have Him indwelling our hearts we can be certain that the work which God has begun in us He will complete in the day of our Lord Jesus Christ (Phil. 1:6).

To sum up then: in Acts we find nothing which leads us to assert a clear position one way or the other. The Corinthian chapters, read in the light of all the Pauline writings, clearly teach the existence of a genuine gift of tongues, but also plainly teach that this gift is not given to every believer, but is just one among a number given sovereignly by God Himself to some and not to others. If we would be true to the New Testament we must not teach anything exclusive or anything that could give rise to a new gnosticism and so divide Christians. The very purpose of the gifts in Scripture is the benefit and edification of the Christian body. Whatever our views then, let us echo the prayer of old John Berridge, 'Lord, if I am right, keep me so; if I am not right, make me so; lead me to the knowledge of the truth as it is in Jesus.'

PART III: STEPHEN

What does it mean to be 'filled with the Spirit'? Whatever may be our convictions about 'the baptism of the Spirit' and 'speaking in tongues' one important truth needs to be stressed: namely, that every true Christian surely longs to enjoy every one of the blessings which the Holy Spirit brings. If the Bible teaches it, we want it! We desire that Paul's great prayer in Ephesians 3:14-21 should be fulfilled in our own experience. Stephen was a man 'filled with the Spirit'. We cannot read about him without wanting to be like him. He stands out as one of the most beautiful and consistent characters in the New Testament—a man that every one of us would like to emulate.

I. STEPHEN'S EXPERIENCE

A practical problem had arisen in the Jerusalem Church and the Apostles were eager that men of certain qualities should be chosen to handle the problem. What they looked for were men 'of good repute, full of the Spirit, and of wisdom'. This implies that not everybody in the Church met this description. These qualifications were not universal in the New Testament Church, even in the early period of the Acts. It is just not true to say that every member of the early Church was full of the Holy Spirit. If it had been so, this instruction would have been meaningless. When the list had been decided, it was headed by Stephen, 'a man full of faith, and of the Holy Spirit', as though he was outstanding in this respect. The names of the others follow. They were chosen because they also fulfilled the conditions but were less outstanding than Stephen. We further read of him that he was 'full of grace and power' and that he 'did great wonders and signs among the people' (Acts 6:8); that 'they could not withstand the wisdom and the Spirit with which he spoke' (v. 10); and that as they gazed at him they saw 'his face was like the face of an angel' (v. 15).

Then follows in chapter 7 his tremendous 'sermon' with its far-sighted realization that, though the Church continued to worship in the temple, the Lord's glory had been revealed not only in the temple, but in many other places as, for instance, to Moses in the Mesopotamian desert. At the end of this marvellous exposition we read, 'But he, full of the Holy Spirit, gazed into heaven and saw the glory of God, and Jesus standing at the right hand of God' (7:55). He himself saw the Shekinah, the glory of God, as it had been revealed in the temple, but now not inside the temple but without, indeed in the very place of execution. Three times in this chapter it is said of Stephen that he was 'filled with the Holy Spirit'. He saw the glory of the Lord which Moses had seen and which in Old Testament days had filled the temple; the glory which Peter, James and John had seen on the Mount of Transfiguration; and the glory which Paul was to see on the Damascus road.

How then are we to understand the statement that Stephen was 'filled with the Holy Spirit'? A doctrine of the fullness of the Holy Spirit is often presented as a universal panacea for all Christian problems. But we can only clearly know what the 'fullness of the Holy Spirit' means by examining the references in the New Testament to this subject.

II. 'FILLED WITH THE SPIRIT'—MEANING OF THE PHRASE

The threefold use of the expression 'filled with the Spirit' with reference to Stephen requires a close examination of the meaning of the phrase elsewhere.

(i) *It is used of a specific experience, on specific occasions, of specific individuals*

Thus it is used of Elizabeth (Luke 1:41) and Zechariah. (Luke 1:67), Peter (Acts 4:8), Stephen here (7:55) and Saul (13:9) before Elymas the sorcerer. In these circumstances, being 'filled with the Spirit' indicated an utterance given through the Spirit in bringing an authoritative and inspired

word of God, be it prophecy, preaching, or judgment. It
was something that happened on specific occasions, and did
not indicate a continuous state. It resembled what happened
in the Old Testament when the Holy Spirit came mightily
upon Saul, Samson or the prophets.

(ii) *It is used of specific experiences, on specific occasions, of specific groups*

The instances are those with the 120 in Acts 2:4 and in
connection with the prayer meeting in Acts 4:31. Again, the
expression does not indicate a continuous state so much as a
remarkable event.

(iii) *It is used of a general condition of individuals*

It was used of John the Baptist (Luke 1:15) as his continuous state from his mother's womb, and of Jesus Himself (Luke 4:1) from the time of His baptism. The experience
of John prevents us from generalizing or drawing too definite conclusions from our Lord's experience. One writer says:
'If Christ needed the baptism of the Holy Spirit who are we
to say that we don't need it?' (John Baker, *Baptized in
One Spirit: the meaning of 1 Corinthians 12:13*, p. 11).
This argument is weighty, but when we note that John the
Baptist was filled with the Spirit from his mother's
womb it makes us cautious of building too much upon
this one Scripture. The expression is also used of the
newly converted Saul (Acts 9:17), of Barnabas (Acts 11:
24), and of the deacons and Stephen in the passage under
consideration.

The New Testament use of the phrase indicates therefore
that it is not true of *all* individual Christians that they are
'filled with the Spirit' and also not true even of the same
individual at *all* times to the same degree. Nevertheless we
would all say, 'O that it may be true of me to the greatest
degree that is possible!' It is surely the longing of every
heart that the things that are said of Stephen might be true
of us: that we may be, in a general sense, men and women
'full of the Spirit and of wisdom': that we may be men 'full

D

of faith and of the Holy Spirit': and that, on particular occasions of great trial, we may be 'full of the Holy Spirit' in a special sense in order to glorify God by word and deed. Our Lord in fact promised this in Mark 13:11: 'Do not be anxious beforehand what you are to say. . . .' It is surely in this sense that we are to understand, 'How much more will the heavenly Father give the Holy Spirit to those who ask him?' (Luke 11:13). That is, we are not to relate those words exclusively to a particular and special second experience called 'the baptism of the Spirit', but to understand them in the sense of a general need which we all have all the time. O that we all might be filled with all the fullness of God! If Scripture did not assure us of such a possibility, we would never dream of asking for such a thing!

III. THE EPHESIAN COMMAND

The classic injunction about being 'filled with the Spirit' is clearly Ephesians 5:18. Probably a great deal has been built upon this verse which cannot really be sustained from the context. The Ephesians references to the Holy Spirit are exceedingly interesting. Each reference to the Holy Spirit in the three doctrinal chapters of the Epistle (ch. 1–3) tells us what God has done for us and our great privileges in Christ: that the Spirit inspires the Word of God, gives access in prayer, is the architect of unity, gives strength, and so on. And then in the three practical chapters of the Epistle (ch. 4–6), our corresponding responsibilities are clearly set out. It is true that the Spirit inspires the Word of God, but our corresponding responsibility is to 'take . . . the sword of the Spirit'. The Holy Spirit gives us access into the presence of God, but we therefore have a corresponding responsibility to use this privilege and to 'pray in the Spirit'. The Holy Spirit is the architect of unity, but we have a corresponding responsibility to maintain the unity of the Spirit in the bond of peace. The Holy Spirit is the one by whom every believer is sealed 'on believing' (1:13)—(the coincident aorist participle again in 'were' sealed); therefore we must not grieve the Spirit by whom we are

sealed (4:30). Our understanding of 'be filled with the
Spirit' (see later, page 55) must be in the light of the
whole Ephesian context, and especially the prayer for
'fulness' in chapter 3:14–21.

IV. THE TREMENDOUS POSSIBILITY—Eph. 3:14–21

(i) *The prayer for strength*

The third chapter of Ephesians contains the glorious
prayer that 'according to the riches of his glory he may
grant you to be strengthened with might through his spirit
in the inner man . . . that Christ may dwell in your hearts
through faith . . . that you may be filled with all the fullness of God'. Whatever our personal conviction may be,
and whether or not we believe in the necessity for a second
special experience subsequent to conversion, sometimes
termed 'the baptism of the Spirit', everyone must surely
desire the experience of being strengthened with might by
His Spirit in the inner man and being filled with all the fullness of God. We should not be satisfied with anything less
than this. If this is what God offers, this is what we want.
The context shows that it is God who does this for us, and
who acts on our behalf. In prayer we express our own weakness and inability and ask Him to strengthen us 'according
to the riches of his glory'.

(ii) *The measure of His strengthening*

The word is not 'from' the riches of His glory, but 'according to'; that is, with a generosity and lavish abundance
worthy of the God of glory. The enduement is appropriate
to God's nature as rich and gracious. If a rich uncle gives a
child sixpence, this would be 'from' or out of his riches, but
it would certainly not be 'according to' or proportionate to
his wealth. 'His glory' suggests the revelation of God's own
intrinsic nature. His promises to strengthen us with might
are consonant with this rich, gracious, abundant, super-
lative nature of His. Where are all the essential abilities,
graces and gifts for our work to come from? From His
character of glory—the glorious wealth of His nature;

from His 'beyond personality' personality—that supra-personality that makes our human persònalities seem so frail and so pale and brittle and thin. Yet this God undertakes to strengthen us 'according to the riches of His glory'.

(iii) *The place of strengthening*

Moreover, He strengthens us 'in the inner man': that is, 'the man within the man' as E. K. Simpson puts it in his commentary on Ephesians. What we expect, therefore, is not the stepping up of the metabolic rate of the outward man which is perishing or fading away fast enough already: not the stepping up of the pace of life into a frantic tarantella of activity like a tadpole immersed in alcohol, but a strengthening of the 'inward man'. We do not merely expect God to use us. The Spirit of the Lord came upon Samson and Gideon and Jephthah and the Lord used them powerfully, but the Scripture suggests that that was something external. The Spirit used to come upon men without necessarily transforming them morally. Gideon could make an ephod and so lead all Israel astray. Jephthah could make a superstitious promise. Samson, a man who was a by-word for strength, could still be a man with an eye for women that ultimately brought him to pitiful weakness. The Spirit came upon their outward man, and God used them. But what Paul prays for the Ephesians is more than this: he prays for a change in the deepest seat of the personality—the inward man. It is not enough for the Spirit to come upon a man, so that he has an 'experience' which may leave him no whit better. The Holy Spirit must strengthen him with might in the innermost being from which He is to cause rivers of living water to flow. Do you fear that hankering after sin in your inward secret heart? Does the Devil tempt you by suggesting that one day you will yield to it and so you might as well give up the struggle now? Are you afraid because corruption remains even in the hearts of those who are regenerate—and so lurks deep in your own heart? Our problems li deep in our inmost being: so this is where we need His grace. Then remember that it is in the innermost heart, the inward man, that the Holy Spirit is able to strengthen us.

(iv) *Strength for the will*

We need strength where we are most weak—in the *will*. William Barclay comments, 'It is the essential weakness of life that so often we know what is right, that we mean to do it, but our will is not strong enough to back our knowledge and carry out our intentions.' Isn't that just our problem? The busy believer has all sorts of things that he wants to do if only he had the will, somehow, to get down to it. Those of us who are busy with many responsibilities have been meaning for a long time to get down to Bible study, or to get on with some active evangelistic witness, or, if we are missionaries, to language study. Others of us have been meaning to speak to a certain person or to start a meeting that has been on our heart for so long. The intention has been there, but our weakness is that while we know what is right and mean to do it, we fail to carry out our intentions. Isn't that one glory of this prayer? The Holy Spirit will strengthen you in your will, for it is God who works in you both *to will* and *to do* of His good pleasure. Are you and I conscious of weaknesses and deficiencies in our inner man? Then let us bring them to Him, as a child runs to his father saying: 'Daddy, this needs mending,' and 'Daddy, I can't do it'! Just as those of us who are fathers say, 'Bring it to me', so does our Heavenly Father invite us to do the same.

(v) *The source of strength*

Notice that Paul says 'strengthened by his Spirit'. He could have said the 'Holy' Spirit, but the words are 'his Spirit', and he adds, 'that Christ may dwell in your hearts' (v. 17). He is making plain that it is the Spirit of God and especially the Spirit of Christ, of Jesus, who dwells in our hearts. The word 'dwell' is the word for permanent residence in contrast to the idea of temporary sojourning (as in 2:19, 'strangers and sojourners'). It is of this Jesus that Paul speaks: the One who did all things well, who fitted so many things into His timetable, who perfectly dealt with the problems and sufferings of all those whom He met. It is *His* Spirit who indwells and strengthens us.

Zen Buddhism has an interesting concept known as the 'cult of spontaneity'. The idea is that by practice and meditation one learns to do things superbly well spontaneously. For example, one can write a Chinese character with a brush in black ink—all in one spontaneous flowing motion. The same is true in Kendo (sword fighting with staves) or in Judo: one can acquire a kind of rapid spontaneous reflex action, much as Europeans admire a quick dummy pass at rugger, or a fast turn in ski-ing. But we Christians, indwelt by the Spirit of Christ and strengthened by His Spirit in the inward man, look for help to act and react as He would act spontaneously doing the right thing, because He Himself dwells within us.

(vi) *The limit of the strength*

'Filled with *all the fullness of God*?' How can such a thing be possible? Unfortunate illustrations about filling empty glasses suggest that the Holy Spirit is a kind of fluid: that it is possible for a Christian to be only half filled! This illustration is only slightly better than those about the glass being full of gas; in which case, of course, the glass is always full, however little else there is in it! These totally inadequate analogies should not distract us from the amazing possibility held out to us. Surely there is no room for all of *Him* in this insignificant *me*? Is not the meaning rather that not just a part of His nature, but every part of Him, every kind of blessing that He can give, can be manifested in my experience; every aspect of His glorious character, His capacity for work, His capacity for love; His capacity for perfect understanding and for doing all things well, His habit of gracious words, and of being 'full of grace and truth'? All that fullness of supra-personality may fill me.

(vii) *The doxology*

But Paul hasn't finished praying yet! In v. 20 he bursts

into a paean of praise—'Him who by the power at work within us is able to do far more abundantly than all that we ask or think.' There are no limits to His ability to bless us. This possibility is so tremendous that it is easy to understand why nobody in the New Testament is ever prepared to claim to be filled with the Holy Spirit. In view of God's greatness, instead of a claim to be in possession of this fullness, there can only be the humble longing to know yet more of Him, and to realize how much more of Him there is for me to experience. Paul does not only say that God is able to do all that we ask or think, but that He is able to do 'above' that; not only so, but 'abundantly' above that; and as if that is not enough, he adds 'exceeding' abundantly above all that we ask or think! Paul piles on the superlatives. If there are any limits to God's ability to bless us then they are infinitely beyond our praying or comprehension. Do we really believe this? A great deal that one hears about 'an experience', and certainly a great deal that one hears from those who oppose 'an experience', comes very, very far short of what the Bible sets before God's people as the limitless possibilities of His blessing.

V. OUR CONSEQUENT RESPONSIBILITY

This is set out in the second half of the epistle (5:18 ff.) beginning with the injunction, 'Be filled with the Spirit'. Stott's booklet has a most helpful exposition of this passage (*The Baptism and Fullness of the Holy Spirit*, p. 28 ff.) He points out that 'being filled' is a main verb and that this main verb is qualified by four auxiliary verbs which, as it were, qualify and explain what 'being filled with the Spirit' means in the context. He notes, too, that the verb is 'present continuous'—and can be translated 'go on being filled'. It is also passive—'let Him fill you'. And it is imperative—something that you must do. The whole verse does not suggest an isolated experience, but something continuous. It does not urge you to seek 'the blessing', after which you have got 'it'. But Paul says that you and I should go on being filled with the Spirit. Finally,

the verb is plural: it is addressed to the whole group of
believers. A contrast is drawn between this experience and
a noisy drunken party—a bad way for a slave to use his
limited free time. What should one do in one's spare time—
go to a drunken party? On the contrary, go to a meeting of
your fellow believers and there be filled with the Spirit! And
when your meeting is filled with the Spirit, in contrast with
a drunken debauch, you will address one another in songs and
hymns and spiritual songs; sing and make melody to the Lord
with all your hearts; always and for everything give thanks,
and be subject to one another out of reverence for Christ.

Such are the marks of being filled with the Spirit in a
Christian gathering. How gratuitous it is, therefore, to take
these verses and apply them to a crisis 'sanctification' experience. Paul describes what the Lord will do for a group of believers as they meet together. This was the experience of the early
Church whenever they met from house to house (Acts 2:42–47).
The Holy Spirit who enables us to sing and make melody to
the Lord with all our hearts (v. 19) is the Holy Spirit who
inspires in us a sense of gratitude, thanksgiving and praise
(v. 20). It is the Holy Spirit who imparts that love of the brethren which enables us to be subject to one another (v. 21).

VI. THE PRACTICAL DAILY REALITY

Paul's prayer contains a wonderful concept of the power of
God, unlimited either by our feeble apprehension or by our
half-hearted prayers. He is able to do exceeding abundantly
above all that we ask or think. It comes almost as an anti-
climax to confront the daily reality of common experience.
If the kind of life Paul describes is possible, why don't we
see more of it? Christians are often so ordinary and so little
different from others. We talk about Christians shining in
the midst of a wicked generation—but do they? Can you
pick out those working on a school or hospital or office staff
who are filled with the light of Christ from those doing the
same job who are not? Perhaps we can, but is the difference
as marked as it should be? Are we as radiant as we long to
be? If we claim to carry the fragrance of the Lord Jesus

with us everywhere, are we as fragrant as we ought to be? Is there some secret which I have yet to learn? Am I deceiving myself in saying how wonderful the Christian life is, when in fact my own experience isn't all that wonderful? I may be a minister, a Christian worker, a missionary, a writer of Christian books, but do I actually experience this unlimited power? We may have met well-known Christian people; but quite honestly, when we get to know them, do we see this unlimited power in their lives? Sometimes we find them to be very ordinary people, little different from ourselves.

Were things different in New Testament times? After Pentecost, although Peter and Barnabas had known the experience of being filled with the Spirit, they were in serious error over fellowship with Gentiles. Being filled with the Spirit did not mean that they were infallible. Paul and Barnabas were men who had been filled with the Spirit, but this did not stop their contention from being sharp. Unwrap the polite language of the Authorized Version and we should read: 'They had a flaming row!' It is important to see the danger of presenting a doctrine in such a way as to suggest that if one is filled with the Spirit, thereafter one lives a life of perfect holiness. Manifestly this was not the case in the New Testament. Although these men knew what it was to be filled by the Holy Spirit they made very serious mistakes, and were capable of having a flaming row. They were far from impeccable!

What then do we mean when we talk about being 'strengthened with his might'? We are familiar with the kind of teaching which says, 'Do you want to be a kind of Christian "superman" with flashing eyes, inexhaustible energy, and a vibrant hypnotic personality? Then seek this experience!' It is possible to be attracted by this undefined 'carrot', without asking whether this is really what the Bible promises. Should someone else offer 'a higher dimension' or a 'deeper experience' through speaking in tongues, we are naturally interested. Even if intellectually we have long believed that the gift of tongues is not for everyone but only for some, we tend to be emotionally attracted by the possibility of a deeper or higher experience. It is therefore very important to seek a definition of what we mean by this higher or deeper dimension. How does the Bible define it? What kind of an experience does the New Testament offer us?

While naturally wanting a deeper experience and a higher dimension, we should beware of thinking of such things in other than strictly Biblical terms. Paul was one who knew what it was to be filled with the Holy Spirit, who apparently spoke in tongues in certain circumstances and who prayed those tremendous prayers recorded in his letters. But of his own experience he writes, 'We have this treasure in earthen vessels, that the exceeding greatness of the power may be of God' (2 Cor. 4:7, *RV*). The exceeding greatness of God's power is there, but the man himself is just an earthen pot. Paul goes on to say: 'We are afflicted in every way . . . perplexed . . . carrying in the body the death of Jesus, so that the life of Jesus may also be manifested in our bodies' (vv. 8–10). Being filled with the Spirit does *not* mean unlimited success. In fact, Paul remains conscious of his inadequacy—'who is sufficient for these things?' (2:16). It is still true that 'his bodily presence is weak, and his speech of no account' (10:10). In other words, it is *God's* power which is unlimited, and not mine. This is an important distinction. The Bible makes it plain that there are one-talent men, two-talent men and five-talent men. There is no limit to the amount of available soil, water and sunlight, but you can never get mustard and cress to grow into a Californian redwood! Trees grow to a certain height, bushes are smaller and annuals are smaller still. Like Paul, God's people may experience failure and be aware of natural limitations.

To take one further example of this principle, the New Testament makes it clear that men filled with the Spirit may still suffer from ill-health. Certainly there is a gift of healing, but it does not follow that it is impossible or even improper for Christians to suffer from the same diseases as other people. Timothy was advised to take a *little* wine for his *frequent* infirmities (1 Tim. 5:23). Epaphroditus (Phil. 2:26, 27) was critically ill apparently for a considerable

period, but there is no record in his case that the gift of
healing was brought into use or that others laid hands on
him. Sickness was a part of Christian experience in the
apostolic age just as it is a part of ours. It is dangerous,
therefore, to contrast a *hypothetical* New Testament ideal
with present experience, and to suggest possibilities for
present experience which were not attained even in New
Testament times.

We all long for a 'higher dimension' and this we shall
experience fully only in heaven. Paul says: 'Now we see
through a glass, darkly; but *then* face to face' (1 Cor. 13:12,
A.V.): 'For we walk by faith, not by sight' (2 Cor. 5:7). There
would be something wrong with us if we were not longing for
a higher and deeper experience; but blessings on earth are
to be defined in New Testament terms. We are not to expect
freedom from all problems, or deliverance from all disasters.
Nor are we necessarily to expect outstanding and continuous evangelistic success. Missionaries who 'speak in tongues'
may still, like Paul, become discouraged or fail language
examinations. It is right that all of us should long for and
seek improvement in ourselves and all the blessings that
there are in Christ. But let us be certain that our expecta-
tions are derived from Scripture.

Unlimited power is found in the electric cables, but a
sixty-watt bulb can burn that much and no more. The
analogy is plain. Some Christians are by nature bright and
others dim. The fullness of the Holy Spirit and the blessing
of God will make a lot of difference as to whether the former
are proud and arrogant or the latter able to compensate in
character for what they lack in gift. In other words, the
power of God is given for purposes clearly defined in Scripture; there are certain natural limits which God has placed
upon each one of us, but His power is available for Christian
living, for Christian courtship, for Christian family life, for
Christian parenthood, for shining like lights, for having a
distinctive saltiness and for being fragrant. All these things
are described in Scripture; for praising God, for worshipping
Him: God's power is available for these things. But it is

not available to make me what God does not purpose for me to be here on earth.

VII. THE APPROPRIATION OF THE POWER

How then may God's power be liberated? In Ephesians 3 Paul is praying for believers. It was suggested earlier that there might be a spiritual secret which we are missing. This is possible, but it is more than probable that it is not so much a new secret as an old one. It is a little like the old lamp which the boy had on his shelf but forgot to use. He became poorer and poorer until the day when almost by accident he rubbed it, and the genii appeared. The riches were there all the time, if only he had asked for them! He did not need some secret new lamp, for the old one in his possession was good enough to make riches available. The secret was in his possession all the time but he was not availing himself of it. Ephesians 3 therefore indicates that *prayer* is the means by which God's power is released in our lives. Private prayer and corporate prayer are the means for obtaining the blessings of God. If we are conscious of living lives which are unsatisfactory, we also know how this state of affairs can be remedied. Our prayers are so often dull, formal and vague. If only they were more definite, specific and realistic! It is possible to pray in a prayer meeting so that the words tumble out, but without seeking anything from the Lord in definite and specific terms, with faith and the expectation that He will answer. God's unlimited power is available for purposes which Scripture defines. It is available so that we may be effective and fruitful, diligent and honest, pure and patient and a blessing to all whom we meet. For such things the power of God is available for the asking. If we want to live like Stephen, and to die like him, then the way to do so is to pray.

To those who are tempted to be critical and unloving towards their brethren who have the experience of speaking in tongues, we must say that these do have a position which may be defended from Scripture, provided the gift is regarded as only for some and not for all. There is nothing divisive in this. Those who stress speaking in tongues also stress prayer. And this is why they are blessed. If they know a new dimension and a new sense of God's blessing it is because they do *pray* and God's blessings are open to everybody who prays. Others of us may prefer to follow Paul's words, 'I will pray with the understanding also', but if so, let us really pray. The reason for dissatisfaction with our experience is usually that we are not praying. God has decreed the way in which we may be 'strengthened with might by his Spirit in the inner man', and 'filled with all the fullness of God'. It is not, through some new secret or some new experience, but through prayer. If our present experience is unsatisfactory it is because we are not, either privately or corporately, the men and women of prayer that we ought to be.

VIII. SOME REMAINING QUESTIONS

Some unanswered questions may still remain in our minds. For example, how should we regard the experience of those who have come to a crisis of yieldedness to God, accompanied by speaking in tongues, which has brought an evident change and lasting blessing into their lives? This experience is distinct from the 'gift of tongues' mentioned in Corinthians. The question touches on the real experimental nub of the problem. First, we must interpret such an experience *Scripturally*, and the Bible clearly teaches that tongues as a gift is for some and not for all. Secondly, we must ask what of those who have come to a crisis of yieldedness to God, bringing an evident change and lasting blessing into their lives, *without* speaking in tongues? It is clear that speaking in tongues may or may not accompany this crisis. Scripturally it is impossible for us to teach that tongues must of necessity accompany such a crisis.

There is the further question for those who have a tongues experience as to how much they should say or teach about it in view of the danger of this being misunderstood and considered divisive. The answer is that we should teach Bible truth in the proportion and in the context of the Bible.

If we do this we shall presumably not teach from 1 Corinthians 12–14 unduly often, and when we do we shall clearly and simply indicate the different possible interpretations of the passage.

It is worth observing, perhaps, that although differences of position over water baptism may generate a good deal of heat between their protagonists, no one is actually 'afraid' of discussing the matter. In regard to 'the baptism of the Spirit' people are often afraid that if they attend a meeting or engage in a discussion related to this subject they will, in spite of their own convictions and indeed against their will, be taken over and as it were 'converted' through some numinous power over which they have no control. It is because of a fear of spiritual and psychic forces present in such meetings or discussions that the matter becomes so divisive. Even medically and psychologically, we are ignorant of many areas of human personality and of psychic forces of various kinds. And for this reason debates on the subject of the 'baptism of the Spirit' are often peculiarly weighted with emotion and with a sense of psychic tension which may result in a feeling of fear. The terrible possibility of being 'inspired' by other than the Holy Spirit Himself (1 Cor. 12:2, 3) is also one from which people naturally shrink. These factors should be recognized as one reason for the over-reaction of some who question the validity of some 'tongues' experiences. Those who claim to have received blessing through such an experience should therefore be sensitive to the cautiousness of others and not necessarily attribute it to a lack of spirituality. If we are all prepared to admit our ignorance about this whole area of human personality, and our ignorance also of what is actually implied or to be understood from some more difficult New Testament passages, then we should be more charitable towards those with whom we disagree and not break fellowship with them. We need to admit readily that, while certain Scriptures *can* be used as support for a particular position, they are also open to other interpretations. We must avoid the dogmatism that says, 'This can mean nothing but . . .' which only aggravates controversy and division. Let us be positive about what Scripture is positive about and where Scripture is patent of differing inter-pretations, it behoves us to be correspondingly cautious and, at the same time, gracious to those with whom we disagree.

'Bless, O gracious Father, thine holy catholic church. Fill it with Thy truth and grace. Where it is corrupt, purge it. Where it is in error, direct it. Where it is superstitious, rectify it; where it is amiss, reform it; where it is right, strengthen and confirm it; where it is divided and rent asunder, heal the breaches of it, O Thou holy One of Israel' (Archbishop Laud).